CURRIES
of the ORIENT

CURRIES
of the ORIENT

by
Harvey Day

HERITAGE PUBLISHERS
15 COMPTON TERRACE
LONDON N1

© 1972 Kaye & Ward Ltd and Heritage Publishers Ltd
Photographs by Angel Studio
Printed in England by Taylowe Ltd, Maidenhead

CONTENTS

I should like to thank
Mrs Margaret Creagan,
a *cordon bleu* in her own
country, for the Burmese recipes
and Mrs Vyvette Loos,
of Negombo, Ceylon, for
the fish curry.   H.D.

1. What makes a curry?

Curries are the traditional foods of India and South-East Asia, compounded of health-giving herbs which are also preservatives. There is no one dish called 'curry': the curries of the different countries and regions are as varied and distinct as the wines of the west. The idea that all curries are fiery enough to burn the skin off one's tongue is sheer nonsense. They range from savoury to very hot and can be made to suit all palates.

How the peoples of the Orient discovered the preservative properties of the herbs will never be known, for curries have been eaten for thousands of years, long before written records were kept. Because of the heat, meat bought in the morning will start to deteriorate and putrefy by evening unless it is curried; then it may be kept for days. Spices from which curries are made were therefore invaluable in the tropics when refrigerators were undreamed of. And in the East, even today, very few people can run to such luxuries.

Hot spices such as chilli and pepper are added to curry herbs specifically to produce perspiration in very hot weather as a means of cooling the skin. Curries are equally useful in cooler climates on very cold days because they produce internal heat; but this does not mean that the curries you cook should be uncomfortably or unbearably pungent. You can make them as hot or as mild as you please.

In Asia very hot curries are usually eaten by the poor who can't afford all the spices needed, for chillis and salt and little else give a kick and piquancy to the cheapest of edibles, such as rice and lentils, which comprise their diet. The pungency of curries depends on the amount of chilli used. If you want to make a curry hotter, add more chilli. If you dislike pungent food, cut it out altogether. And if you

7

patronize a curry restaurant, ask if the dishes are very hot and tell them of your preference. Many in their excusable ignorance wade through a meal that is much too hot and vow never to touch curries again.

Immense variety

Not surprisingly, curries differ widely throughout the Orient, and even within India and Pakistan. (Strictly speaking there is no such thing as Pakistani cookery: Pakistan did not exist as a separate entity until 1947, and really its food is Moslem cookery that has been influenced by Turkish, Persian and Afghan cuisine.) Strict Hindus are vegetarian and specialize in cakes of wheat and various grains; in rice prepared in a score of different ways; in curries called *bhajjis* made from vegetables and eaten with chutneys, pickles, oil, vinegar, salt, mustard and yogurt.

Moslems, on the other hand, are great meat-eaters. Their food is much drier, often rendering knives and forks superfluous. In their meat recipes one is told to *bogharer* the meat; that is, fry it before cooking in spices, an operation which transforms a merely tasty dish into one that is delicious. Their cuisine also includes many Persian dishes: the *pilao,* which has rice as its base and is cooked in *ghee* (clarified butter) or butter, is heavily spiced and sometimes contains sultanas, raisins and almonds; the *birianee,* whcih is a cross between a *pilao* and a curry; *ashes,* which contain meat, flour, lentils and vegetables, and even fruit, sugar, milk and yogurt; *kababs,* consisting of meat and vegetables heavily spiced, cut into slices or chunks, or moulded into segments, and then skewered on wooden, steel or wire skewers and grilled over an open fire.

The Bangladeshis specialize in fish and bamboo curries cooked in mustard oil, flavoured with coconut milk and eaten with rice. In Burma, Ceylon, Indonesia and Indo-China, fish curries also predominate, as water is rarely more than a stone's throw away and fish plentiful. Coconut milk nearly always accompanies fish. A favourite fish in Ceylon is the shark, often eaten with screw pine and lemon grass. In Malaysia and Indo-China are many fish not known in European waters: *bawal tambak, senangin, tenngiri, kurau, chermin, parang-parang, terubok, janahak, siakap,* and other smaller varieties such as *selar, kembong, chencharu, selangat, puput* and *tamban.* Where coconut milk is used with fish, curries never contain cummin and coriander, as these destroy their delicate flavour.

Malaysian, Indonesian and Indo-Chinese cookery is much influenced by Chinese cookery. This leads to the use of bean sprouts and soya sauce, and also of *blachan,* known in India and Burma as *ballychow. Blachan* is made from prawns or shrimps, salted, dried, pounded and rotted, and shaped into cakes. The process sounds neither hygienic nor appetizing, but none are the worse for eating it and millions regard it as a delicacy, which indeed it is. It is no worse than grouse that is 'high', or 'ripe' cheese like Limburger. In parts of Burma fish is buried for three weeks before being compounded into *ballychow! Blachan* is fried in a little fat or oil, but under the guise of *ballychow* it takes the form of a thick paste and may be bought in bottles and used without further preparation.

Curry ingredients

A word about the ingredients of curry. A glance at the chapter of recipes will show that not all curries are made in the same way. They may be made either from paste or from powder. In Asia, where the spices may be bought fresh every day, they are usually ground into a paste on a large, flat stone base, using a small cylindrical stone for grinding. But elsewhere curry powders are the most convenient way, unless one buys proprietary curry pastes in bottles. These are expensive, and the most expensive way is not always the best.

You can buy curry spices and make your own powders, altering the ratio of the various ingredients to suit your palate, and in this way get an infinite variety of flavours. You can grind dried chilli, ginger, peppercorns, cardamom, cinnamon, cummin, mustard seed etc in a coffee grinder–

9

though, after grinding, plenty of hard bread or toast, or some other neutral substance, should be passed through the grinder, which will otherwise smell of curry spices.

Don't be afraid to make powders in quantity. Provided you store them in glass jars with hermetically sealed stoppers, such as Kilner jars, their fragrance will improve with time; but if air can get in they will deteriorate.

The following are the principal curry ingredients:

Common name	Botanical name
aniseed	*Pimpinella anisum*
allspice	*Myrtus pimenta*
cardamom	*Elelbaria cardamomum*
mace	*Myristica moschata*
nutmeg	*Myristica moschata*
cinnamon	*Laurus cinnamomum*
coriander	*Coriandrum sativum*
cloves	*Engenia caryophyllata*
cummin	*Cuminum cyminum*
black pepper	*Piper nigrum*
mustard seed	*Sinopis sinensis*
chilli	*Capsicum frutescens*
turmeric	*Curcuma longa*
fenugreek	*Trigonella foenum craecum*
garlic	*Alium sativum*
ginger	*Amomum zingiber*
poppy seed	*Papaver somniferum*
long pepper	*Piper longum*
asafoetida	*Ferula asafoetida*
chironji nut	*Buchanonia latifolia*
almond	*Amygdalia communis*
coconut	*Cocus nucifera*

All the spices listed are good for health when consumed in small quantities or in combination with other spices and foods:

Aniseed has an aromatic odour, warms the stomach, is a carminative and is used as a remedy for colic and eradicates harmful intestinal bacteria.

Allspice is an appetizer and contains vitamin C. It is an aromatic stimulant, carminative and used in tonics.

Cardamom warms the stomach, is a carminative, and 2 ounces of crushed cardamom in a pint of boiling water, strained and taken in wineglass doses when cool, removes flatulence. All over the East a few cardamom seeds are usually eaten after a meal as a digestive.

Nutmeg and **mace** both contain a volatile oil which is used in cases of renal or hepatic colic, and for certain nervous maladies. Mace lends fragrance and is an appetizer. Nutmeg oil aids the digestion, is carminative, helps to stop vomiting, and is sometimes given in cases of dysentery and to counteract the effects of certain poisons.

Cinnamon is an extremely powerful germicide. Some years ago the scientist Cavel infected beef tea with water taken from the collecting tank of a sewage system. To one sample was added cinnamon oil diluted to 4 parts in 1,000; to another oil of cloves diluted to 2 parts in 1,000. The germs in each sample were destroyed. When carbolic acid was used the strength of the solution had to be increased to 5·6 parts in 1,000 to be equally effective.

Coriander is aromatic and a carminative. It is pungent and used to make a cordial, the best known being the renowned Eau de Carmes, first prepared in the Middle Ages in the pharmacy of the Carmelite monks from lemon peel, coriander seed, nutmeg, cloves, cinnamon, angelica root and spirits of wine. It warms the stomach, strengthens the heart and allays gripping caused by laxatives.

Cloves–the entire tree, not only the fruit, has a smell that refreshes the weary. It is the most stimulating of all aromatic spices and when made into a cordial warms, strengthens the stomach, soothes and stimulates at the same time. It is highly antiseptic and clove tea has been taken to relieve nausea. A mixture of cloves, allspice, ginger and cinnamon infused with a little brandy and warmed by the sun gives instant relief in cases of colic.

Cummin is carminative and the strongest of all ground spices. It is appetizing and antiseptic and forms the basis

11

of almost all Indian curries.

Black pepper–the peppers have been used for centuries because of their medicinal properties. Black pepper was administered to fever patients in doses of 6-10 grains in the form of pills. It does not suppress fever as quinine does but causes the patient to perspire profusely. Unlike fevers cured by quinine, these do not recur and there are no harmful effects such as deafness. Rich in vitamin C.

Mustard– there are two kinds, white and black; the white is a small plant and is grown with cress to make mustard-and-cress. The black is stronger, has medicinal properties and contains sulphur. It is used in curries to counteract dyspepsia. The seeds or powder are used in curries and in some areas the oil is used to cook the curries in. In *Diet and Reform* M. K. Gandhi says that mustard contains 98-99% fat and traces of manganese, nickel and cobalt.

Chilli is a fine stimulant, a carminative, tonic, diaphoretic and rubefacient. It produces a natural warmth and uniform circulation. Taken in small quantities in combination with other herbs it strengthens the heart.

Turmeric is widely used in the East for skin diseases, healing bruises and leech bites, and is a carminative.

Fenugreek–a poultice of fenugreek is excellent for wounds; a tea made from it is a good gargle for sore throats. Good for fevers.

Garlic is the queen of curry spices. Both onions and garlic are blood cleansers and ward off colds in winter. In some European countries both are eaten raw. Garlic is rich in vitamins B, C and D, and onion in C. Recently it was discovered that an insecticide made from garlic kills up to 98% of all known pests, yet is harmless to people and animals. As an internal cleanser garlic has few equals. Experiments carried out at the University of California have proved that onions contain allyl aldehyde and garlic crotonic aldehyde, both potent germ destroyers. Both are rich in the trace elements zinc, copper, aluminium, manganese, sulphur and iron which, scientists have now discovered, help to keep away disease.

Ginger has for centuries been used as a medicine by

Chinese and Indians and is mentioned in Chinese medical works, in Sanskrit literature and in the Talmud, the body of Jewish law. It is said to have aphrodisiac properties and was highly esteemed by, among others, King Henry VIII of England. In Britain ginger wine is still taken as a cordial for keeping out the cold.

Poppy seed enters largely into Indian, Russian, Hungarian and Jewish cuisine because of the aromatic oil which gives a distinctive taste and aroma and for its vitamin and protein content.

Long pepper–the entire pepper family, which includes capsicum, African pepper, bird pepper, Guinea pepper and chillis, adds piquancy and pungency to food, and if taken in *small* quantities is a heart stimulant, not a drug. In addition the peppers are rich in vitamin C, are carminative, tonic, diaphoretic and rubefacient.

Asafoetida adds taste and contains vitamin C.

Chironji nut lends variety and has a high protein content.

Almond is used mainly in Indian sweets and *pilaos,* and for garnishing. Contains more protein than beef (21·70%), 54·40% fat, 18·80% carbohydrates and 2·40% mineral matter. Almonds have an alkali base, so are not acid-forming.

Coconut both the flesh and the milk are used. In South India, Ceylon and most of South-East Asia, coconut oil is used for cooking. The flesh is used in making sweets and the milk adds flavour to curries that nothing else can impart.

Fats to use

In South-East Asia, as we have just seen, coconut oil is the commonest cooking fat. In northern India *ghee* and mustard oil are the main fats. *Ghee* is clarified butter: that is, butter treated with steam to remove impurities. It tastes quite different from butter. Mustard oil should always be heated till a wisp of blue smoke rises from the surface before adding ingredients, otherwise the curry will taste of it.

Where Chinese influence is strong, lard is used: and

some Chinese sweets, such as *Ba Bo Fan* (Eight Treasures Rice Pudding), use four tablespoons of lard to two cups of glutinous rice!

For the best results at home use *ghee,* butter, mustard oil or olive oil, though in the East olive oil is never used. Lard, dripping, peanut oil, coconut oil, soya bean oil or any of the proprietary oils on the market may also be used.

Men in the Orient like their women plump, with well moulded limbs–something they can get hold of; and in India and Pakistan the terms 'fat' and 'strong' are often synonymous. As a result people eat more fatty foods than in the West. The idea that women should slim is abhorrent. On the other hand my wife, who has put on no more than seven pounds in thirty years, has experimented for some time making curries without the use of any fat whatever, and to both of us they taste no worse than curries made with fat!

So those who love curries but fear to eat them because of their fatty content can do likewise. Where in the preparation of curry ingredients the reader is told to fry onions, garlic and curry spices in oil, butter or fat, he should use instead a little *boiling* water–and he will find to his delight that there is no loss of flavour or aroma, and no layer of oil floating on top when the curry is cold. In any case, if the curries are made properly this last should not happen: nonetheless it sometimes does.

Fat must be used, however, in frying meat balls for instance, in making *pilaos* and in certain other dishes.

2. All about rice

Rice to the Oriental is what bread is to the Westerner, who eats bread daily and never tires of it. The Oriental eats rice every day and it sustains him, for rice contains 8% protein and nearly 80% carbohydrates–and unpolished rice has nearly three times the mineral matter of polished rice.

Thus rice firstly provides nutrition and secondly acts, like bread, as a filler. A third purpose is to neutralize excessive pungency, and to help bring out the flavours of various dishes. A little curry from one dish can be placed on an area of virgin rice; then a little curry from another on another free area, and so on. In this way two, three or even more curries may be sampled in the same meal, and more eaten of those you like.

There is more than one kind of rice: stubby-grained 'table rice' from Carolina; long thin rice from Patna and even thinner from Kashmir; Burma rice; *pilao* rice; Chinese rice etc. The best general type of rice for use with curries is Patna, which can be had at any good grocer.

By far the commonest way of cooking rice is to boil it. There are, however, other ways, used especially in India and Pakistan: it may be cooked with lentils under the name of *khichiri* (kedgeree); or fried in butter or *ghee* and interlarded with spices, raisins and nuts and known as *pilao;* or cooked with all these, together with meat and vegetables and called *biriunee,* or made into sweet dishes with milk and spices; or used in a delicious Indian soup called mulligatawny, famous throughout the world–though the *mulegootunne* of South India bears little relation to the product we buy in cans.

Rice, in short, is one of the easiest and quickest dishes to cook and, when well made, delicious. When you have cooked your rice in some of its many forms you may even grow to be an addict. And now we hope to initiate you into some of its mysteries.

Plain boiled rice

Rice should be cooked till each grain is dry and firm and separate from all the others, for nothing puts one off rice dishes so much as lumpy, clogging, soggy rice. It's easy enough as long as someone hasn't already convinced you it's an incredibly complicated ritual. Here are two ways of boiling rice.

Method I: Cover the rice in water *once* and drain it. Then three-quarters fill a large saucepan with water. Add a teaspoon of salt if you wish–most people do, though we do not, and guests at our board seem not to notice the lack of it (and rheumatic sufferers and those afflicted by high blood pressure or heart complaints should avoid it)–and sprinkle in as much rice as you need. One breakfast cup full should be more than enough for two, for rice swells alarmingly. You may bring the water to the boil before sprinkling in the rice, or you may start the water from cold. It doesn't matter one way or the other. You may simmer the rice for 15-20 minutes or boil it hard for 10. It depends on the time at your disposal and the other things you have to do in the kitchen. There is no mystique about the business.

What is important is this: note when the grains begin to swell, then take out one or two and test between finger and thumb. If they are still hard, cook a little longer before testing again. When they are soft but *firm* take the pan off the stove, place it under a tap and pour in cold water. This separates the grains from each other. Now strain off into a sieve or colander. Then shake the rice into a warmed dish. Riffle lightly with a fork to let the air circulate and set the dish in a warm place (such as a pre-heated oven) but not on a flame. If in an oven, keep the door ajar and cut off the heat. In 5-10 minutes the rice should be ready to serve.

By following these directions those who have hitherto turned out a gluey

Vietnamese meat curry (p. 36). Coconut milk gives it its own flavour.

mess will produce a pile of firm, snowy, appetizing grains.

A word of warning: *don't* cook the grains until you can press them into a mash between finger and thumb, or a mash will result. Make sure that the inner core is still firm. Under-cooking is preferable to over-cooking as far as rice is concerned.

Method II: Measure with cups the quantity of rice needed. Then measure accurately twice that volume of water. Place rice and water in a *thick*-bottomed pan and soak for at least 30 minutes.

Bring the water to the boil, then turn down the heat and simmer *very gently* till every particle of water has been absorbed. When this is done the rice should be perfectly cooked and each grain separate from the others. Make sure that you use a pan with a tightly fitting lid; otherwise too much steam will escape, the rice will not be quite cooked through by the time the water has evaporated, and you will have to add more water.

The disadvantage of this method for the figure-conscious is that the starch which went down the drain when the rice was strained in Method I is here retained, and adds considerably to both the calorific value and starch content.

Nutritional value of rice
Much of the rice eaten in the East has a tissue-like red covering, such as one finds on peanuts. This skin is rich in aneurin or vitamin B_1, which prevents the disease beri-beri. If one's diet consists mainly of rice, as is the case with millions of poor all over the East, then this skin must be retained–otherwise one falls a prey to deficiency diseases. However, one of the habits the Europeans took with them to the East was that of polishing rice, which removes the red husk and with it the goodness. For unpolished rice contains 17 I.U. (International Units) of vitamin A, 15 I.U. of vitamin B_1 and $1 \cdot 00\%$ mineral matter; whereas polished rice is devoid of vitamins A and B_1 and contains only $0 \cdot 35\%$ mineral matter.

I know a man who washes his rice eighteen times before

using it. Don't do it. There was a monastery in Saigon next door to a nunnery; and both monks and nuns ate the same rice. French doctors were puzzled, however, because they could not explain why the nuns contacted beri-beri, whereas the monks remained in rude health. It wasn't till later that a Dutchman named Kuenen discovered, purely by accident, that if rice is rinsed many times the protective coats are as effectively removed as if the grains had been polished. So the dirty monks who did not believe in such niceties as washing their rice remained free from disease, while the ultra-clean nuns fell victims. The moral is that you can be too hygienic!

On their meagre diet of red rice and, when they can run to it, a handful of lentils and a few vegetables, the very poor of the East perform miracles of stamina. The rice-eating peoples are usually short in stature and have a delicate bone structure. They may not have the sheer brute strength that Westerners possess, but their stamina is impressive. When the American forces went to India in 1943 they were staggered to behold rickety-looking coolies heaving immense loads onto their heads and loping off with them.

There may be some element in rice, which so far we have not been able to isolate, that provides stamina. Dr Robert Runnel Williams, the first man to extract pure vitamin B_1 oil from rice bran and feed it to a child in Malaysia who suffered from pain in the heart and intestines and was dying from beri-beri, is sure that the thin red coating on rice strengthens the heart and provides the surprising stamina of the rice-eating races, who in their own countries rarely suffer from heart diseases.

3. Ways with lentils

Lentils form the main protein food of millions in the East but are not as widely used in the West as they might be because we have so many alternative protein foods and are much more partial to meat than the peoples of the East.

Lentils and their relatives are eaten throughout India, Pakistan and Asia in general, cooked in a variety of ways. In China, for instance, a banquet from soup to sweet can be served, made entirely of soya bean, and the diner is led to believe he is tasting fish, flesh, fowl and sweet!

However, lentils are particularly a feature of North Indian cooking for they need a fairly dry, hot climate, though lentil dishes in Malaysia and Indonesia have been grafted on to the indigenous cuisine by Moslem immigrants. The reasons why India has such a variety of lentil and bean dishes are (1) India is largely vegetarian, (2) many of her people are poor and pulses are cheap, easily grown in a tropical climate and do not need manuring, (3) they are extremely sustaining, (4) they can be eaten alone or as an accompaniment and (5) they can be made into sweets.

The lentil is therefore an all-purpose food which gives more nourishment for a smaller outlay of cash than any other comestible. Indeed, of all the foods known to man, pulses have the highest protein value–even surpassing meat in many instances. Because of their concentrated protein content they should be eaten sparingly, and to avoid indigestion no more than 2-3 ounces (uncooked, dry weight) should be consumed in a day.

In more detail, lentils contain 12·35% water, 25·70% protein, 1·90% fat, 53·30% carbohydrate and 3·04% mineral matter consisting of potassium, sodium, calcium, manganese, iron, phosphorus,

Ceylon chicken curry (p. 39). Whole chicken joints are used and served on the bone.

sulphur and chlorine. The mineral matter is also higher than in any flesh food, fish or poultry, and they are also rich in vitamins A, B_1 and B_2.

Delicious, nutritious, time-saving soups may be concocted from lentils and make meals in themselves.

Here are three.

Lentil Soup (I)

1 breakfast cup lentils	1 ham bone
1 carrot, grated	2 large onions, finely sliced
Salt and pepper to taste	

Bring 4 pints of water *to the boil,* put in all the ingredients and after 2 minutes lower heat and simmer for 2 hours. Serve with (preferably) 100% wholemeal bread, plain or buttered, or toast the bread, cut into ½-inch cubes and float on the soup. Enough for two.

Lentil Soup (II)

1 cup lentils	1 teaspoon cummin
1 turnip	1 teaspoonful coriander
1 blade mace	¼ teaspoon turmeric
6 cups stock or water	6 peppercorns
1 large carrot	1 tablespoon lentil flour
1 large onion	1 tablespoon dripping
1 small onion	Salt to taste

Melt dripping in a deep pan. Chop vegetables (except the small onion) and add; then lentils; stir till dripping has been absorbed. Add stock (and a bone if you have one), peppercorns and salt to taste. Bring mixture to the boil, then lower heat and simmer for 2 hours. Put through a hair sieve.

Finely slice the small onion, add cummin, coriander and turmeric and cook on a medium heat for 3 minutes, mixing the whole time. Then add the flour with a little milk, stir and boil for 2-3 minutes and while hot add to soup. Serve with *Burmese vegetable curry (p.39). Overleaf: Indian Koaftah (meatball)curry (p.30) with poppadams, Bombay duck, khichiri etc.*

22

wholemeal bread or toast. Lentil flour, or *basoon,* can be bought in Indian spice shops.

Lentil Soup (III)

1 breakfast cup lentils	*2 large onions, sliced*
½ teaspoon cummin	*3 cloves garlic*
Salt to taste	*A shake of pepper*

Fry onions in a little cooking fat till golden. Chop the garlic and add it to the mixture, then stir in cummin and cook rapidly for 2 minutes. Take pan off heat and set aside.

Bring 2 pints of water *to the boil,* toss in the lentils, pepper and salt and boil rapidly for 2-3 minutes, then simmer gently for 20, when the lentils should be soft. Whisk till the lentils are completely broken up and, while still simmering, add the fried onion, garlic and cummin. Garnish with finely chopped parsley and serve with wholemeal bread. Enough for two.

Khichiri

Finally, to return to lentils in Indian cookery, here is a recipe for *khichiri,* or kedgeree, which is often eaten with curries instead of plain boiled rice:

1 lb rice	*1 tablespoon oil or fat*
½ lb lentils	*½ teaspoon cummin seed*

Cook rice and lentils in 3 pints of water till lentils are soft. If the water is boiling before the lentils are put in, they will soften much more quickly than if the water is cold or tepid.

Heat the fat in a frying pan and drop in the cummin seed, which will soon start popping and jumping with the heat. The moment it does, take the pan off the stove and pour the fat over the rice and lentils. Mix thoroughly.

Khichiri may be eaten with curries or with yogurt and mango or lemon pickle.

Indian beef curry cooked with vegetables (p. 28).

4. Selected curry recipes

This chapter contains twelve recipes: two each from India, Pakistan, Ceylon, Burma, Malaysia and Vietnam. Both recipes from each country are based on the same curry powder, details of whose ingredients will be found on page 45. Once you have tried them you can of course experiment with making up powders in different combinations, remembering that the mildness or pungency of a curry is basically determined by the amount of chilli. Using the ingredients as suggested in this book, the order of strength from mild to hot is: Pakistan, India, Burma, Vietnam, Malaysia, Ceylon.

Garlic and/or onions form the basis of most curries. I repeat: don't be afraid to use them freely. When cooked they do not taint the breath and garlic, in particular, can make the world of difference between a good curry and an almost tasteless one.

India (I): Beef Curry

2 lb lean beef	2 large onions
Salt to taste	Indian curry powder

Cut the beef into 1-inch cubes. Slice onions finely and fry to a light brown in a tablespoon of oil. Mix the powder into the onions and cook briskly for 4 minutes. Now add the beef and mix thoroughly. Add a cupful of water and cook for 10 minutes, then put in any vegetables you fancy: small potatoes, diced carrots, cauliflower etc. Just cover with water, bring to the boil, then lower the heat and simmer until meat is tender. Eat with rice, *chappattis* or *parattas,* with or without pickle. Mutton, pork, veal or chicken may be substituted for beef. Enough for four.

Ceylon fish curry (p.33). Contains dark sugar.

28

India (II): Koaftah Curry

2 lb beef, finely minced	2 green chillis, finely chopped
2 large onions, finely chopped	8 cloves garlic, finely chopped
4 medium-sized potatoes, well mashed	6 tomatoes, finely chopped
2 eggs	1 cup coconut milk
Squeeze of lemon	1½ teaspoons salt
Indian curry powder	

Mix thoroughly the chillis, potatoes, meat, 1 teaspoon of
curry powder and 1 teaspoon salt and blend with the eggs.
With lightly floured fingers form the meat into balls the
size of apricots. Fry them to light brown in cooking fat,
then drain off the fat.

Use some of the drained fat to fry the onions, garlic and
tomatoes, and add to them the remaining curry powder.
Cook lightly for a further 5 minutes, then add the coconut
milk, ½ teaspoon salt and a generous squeeze of lemon.

Mix all the ingredients together and simmer *gently* for
30 minutes, shaking the pan gently from time to time to
ensure that they do not stick or burn. Serve with rice and
either chutney or pickle. Enough for four.

Pakistan (I): Pilao Sindhi–style

2 lb meat, cut into chunks	½ lb Patna rice
4 onions, finely sliced	½ lb cooking fat
1 teaspoon salt	Pakistan curry powder

Place the powder in a small muslin bag and put it and the
meat into a pan containing 2 pints of water. Bring to the
boil and simmer till meat is tender.

Fry onions to a deep brown in fat and then put in rice and
salt. Fry for 10 minutes more over a brisk *Pakistan Mutter*
flame, than add meat and broth. Stir well, *pilao (p. 33).*
add more salt if needed, and a cup of milk. *Nuts and parsley*
The rice will soon absorb the liquid; if you *add interest and*
think there is not sufficient to cook the *flavour.*

rice without burning it, add a little more water or milk. Cook on a very low heat till rice is soft: cooking time should be roughly 1½ hours. Enough for four.

Pakistan (II): Mutter Pilao

½ lb Patna rice	1½ lb fresh or canned peas
4 oz cooking fat	2 onions, sliced finely
½ teaspoon salt	Pakistan curry powder

Fry onions to a golden brown in fat, then add salt and powder and continue to fry until onions are well browned. Wash rice and peas and add them to the onions: fry for 10 minutes. Now pour in 2 pints of boiling water and cook over a very low flame till the rice is soft but each grain still separate.

Total cooking time 45 minutes. Fried potato or fried cauliflower may be used instead of peas. Enough for two.

Ceylon (I): Fish Curry

2 lb fish	10 small onions, sliced
1 dessertspoon 'foot' sugar	2-3 fennel leaves, chopped
1 tablespoon vinegar	1 tablespoon cooking oil
Ceylon curry powder	

Wash and cut the fish into pieces. Put into a pan, add a little water, vinegar and salt and boil for 5 minutes. Then remove from stove.

Heat oil and brown onions, then put in the fish, the curry powder, the fennel leaves, the rest of the vinegar and water as necessary and boil for 10 minutes without covering the pan. Just before removing from the stove add the sugar, which conveys a distinctive tang. Serve with lime pickle. Enough for four.

'Foot' sugar is a very dark variety. If unobtainable use molasses or 'pieces', which may be had from almost any grocer.

Malaysian satai or kabab (p. 35). The pineapple is not essential but adds a typical flavour.

33

Ceylon (II): Chicken Curry

1 chicken	*6 onions, sliced*
2-3 fennel leaves, chopped	*1 tablespoon vinegar*
1 tablespoon cooking oil	*Salt to taste*
Ceylon curry powder	

Wash the chicken and cut into joints. Heat the fat, brown the onions, then put in the curry powder, vinegar and fennel leaves and cook rapidly for 5 minutes. Then put in the chicken pieces.

When well fried, add a breakfast cup of water and salt to taste (and a cup of coconut milk if desired). If tamarind is obtainable, boil a quarter pod (the tamarind is a bean) in a little water and add. Eat with rice and pickle. Enough for four.

Burma (I): A Mair Hnut (beef curry)

2 lb beef	*4 medium-sized onions*
4 oz yogurt	*1 tea cup cooking oil*
½ teaspoon shrimp paste or powder	*Burma curry powder*

Cut the beef into 2-inch cubes. Pound onions into a pulp. Mix in the powder, the shrimp paste or powder and the beef, then add oil and yogurt.

Do this the night before you intend to cook the dish, as the mixture has to stand for at least 8 hours.

Next day add ½ cup of water, bring to the boil, then turn down heat *very low* and simmer gently till meat is tender and the oil rises to the surface. If it tends to boil dry, add water. Eat with lime or other pickle. Enough for four.

Burma (II): Vegetable Curry

Enough vegetables for four	*3 medium-sized onions*
1 lemon	*½ tea cup cooking oil*
Salt to taste	*Burma curry powder*

Clean, peel and cut vegetables into 1½-inch pieces. Slice the onions thinly. Mix together onions, oil, powder and salt to taste. Fry briskly for 5 minutes, then add vegetables. Just cover with water and simmer till vegetables are soft. Add lemon juice before serving.

The best vegetables to use are tomatoes, peas, beans, cauliflower and small potatoes.

Eat with or without pickle. Enough for four.

Malaysia (I): Chicken Gravy Curry

6 small cucumbers or a quarter of a small white pumpkin	4 teaspoons pulped onion
1 chicken	2 blades lemon grass or bay leaf
2 cups coconut milk	Salt to taste
Malaysia curry powder	

If using pumpkin, skin it, remove the seeds and cut into 16 pieces about 2 inches square. If cucumbers, don't peel but cut into 2-inch rounds. Either way, steep in water for an hour.

Mix onion and powder and fry in a little cooking fat. When brown add the chicken, cut into pieces. Salt to taste.

Drain the pumpkin or cucumber and add. Pour in coconut milk and lemon grass or bay leaves. Bring to the boil then turn down the heat at once and simmer gently for an hour, when the chicken should be tender. Remove lemon grass or bay leaves before serving. Enough for four.

Malaysia (II): Satai or Kabab

2 lb fatty beef	4 teaspoons pulped onion
Salt to taste	Malaysia curry powder

Cut the beef into 1-inch cubes and baste in oil. Remove the beef.

Put curry powder and onion into the oil and fry briskly till brown. Roll the beef in this sauce till it is thoroughly impregnated, then skewer the bits of meat on to a thin steel needle (such as a knitting needle) and grill over a powerful heat so that the inside is soft and the outer edges are crisp. Usually eaten with *chappattis* or *parattas*. Enough for four.

Vietnam (I): Liver Curry

2 lb sliced liver	2 teaspoons fried onion flakes
2 tablespoons peanut butter	1 teaspoon brown sugar
2 cups coconut milk	2 tablespoons soya sauce
2 bay leaves	Salt to taste
Vietnam curry powder	

Sauté the onions in a little oil. Add the curry powder, peanut butter, bay leaves and sugar. Stir. Now add liver, soya sauce and salt and cook for 5 minutes. Then reduce heat and add coconut milk. Continue cooking and stir continuously till the liquid thickens. Serve hot with rice and top with onion flakes. Enough for four.

Vietnam (II): Meat with Coconut Milk

2 lb steak	2 large onions, grated
6 teacups coconut milk	Salt to taste
Vietnam curry powder	

Put the coconut milk and the curry powder into a saucepan and bring to the boil. Add meat, cut into 2-inch cubes, and salt to taste. Cook on a low heat till milk is absorbed; then stir with a wooden spoon till oil is released from the coconut milk – but do not stir before milk is absorbed as the meat will disintegrate. The dish should be fairly dry. If you want gravy, remove the pan from the stove before the liquid is absorbed. Serve with rice and pickle. Enough for four.

5. Indian bread

We have already seen that rice is the Asian equivalent of our bread: the staple food and the filling that accompanies curries. No wheat is grown in South-East Asia, so bread is not eaten there.

In India, however, where wheat is abundant, a variety of excellent breads are made, as also in Malaysia, into which some wheat is imported. Until the advent of the British, bread made with yeast was virtually unknown in India. Unleavened bread was eaten, and it still is by the greater part of the population.

Westerners who have made its acquaintance in India like it, but it is rarely seen in Western homes, and a mystery surrounds the making of it. In fact it is much easier to make than Western bread and is a natural accompaniment to curries.

Chappattis

For every pound of wholemeal flour – and *chappattis* are made of nothing else – you need approximately 1 cup of water.

Mix flour, water and a pinch of salt to a fairly stiff dough. Knead it well. Pinch pieces off the dough and mould them into balls the size of a walnut. Sprinkle flour on a table or rolling board and roll each ball out to the thickness of a pancake.

Place a large frying pan, *ungreased,* on the stove and heat it. Then place the *chappatti* in the pan and fry for about 2 minutes on each side. Remove, apply a little melted butter on each side and fry again to a brown colour. Eat while hot, either plain or with curry. *Chappattis* may also be made with rice flour, or with a mixture of flour and sweet potato.

Parattas

Parattas are usually made with white flour into which *ghee* and water are mixed. The Indian way is to take a little ball of the mixture, press it flat and throw it from one palm to the other till it grows to the size of a dinner plate. It is then thrown on to a heated, inverted iron bowl and fat is spread over it with a tiny mop, at which it fluffs up. It is quickly turned, the other side similarly treated, and the *paratta* is whisked off the griddle. The entire operation from start to finish takes about a minute: the *paratta* is placed on a leaf; a skewer of *kabab* is placed in the middle; the leaf is folded and pinned with a tooth-pick; and the hot meal is handed to the waiting customer. The art is not easily acquired.

Poorees

Mix wholemeal flour as you would for *chappattis;* add a little fat but use less water. Pinch off little pieces, mould into balls the size of marbles and roll out flat into cakes about 4 inches in diameter. Heat a chip pan or frying pan with oil, butter or margarine, and when the fat is really hot pop in a little cake, which will swell within seconds. When it is light brown, turn and do the other side. Drain and eat hot, either plain or with curry.

Poorees are easily made and stuffed ones are delicious. All you do is roll the *pooree* to a slightly larger size, drop the stuffing on to half one side, fold over and pinch down. Then cook precisely as above. Any stuffing will do: chopped meat (ham, bacon, leftovers), lentils, potato etc.

Poppadams

Poppadams, which may be bought in tins or packets, look like large biscuits about 5 inches in diameter and much thinner. Butter each side *very lightly* and put the *poppadam* under a glowing grill. Watch it, because in a few seconds the *poppadam* will swell. As soon as it turns a golden brown, turn and do the other side. Remove at once. It should be crisp and crackly and is excellent when eaten with curry and rice.

6. A variety of side dishes

Accompaniments to curries range from the simple to the quite complex. Among the former are fruits: pineapple, a favourite in Malaysia, goes very well. Also common all over South-East Asia are onion chips. These are onions sliced in rounds, fried till crisp and brown and sprinkled as a garnish over rice.

Throughout India, Burma and Ceylon, Bombay duck *(sootkie)* is highly esteemed. This is not a bird, but is made from cured *blomboe* fish which, uncooked, has an offensive odour. Cooking transforms it. Toast or grill the fish till they begin to curl, and then crumble and sprinkle them over rice, or crunch them as you would a stick of celery with each mouthful of curry and rice. Don't be put off by the smell: give them a trial. They can be bought in grocers or Indian food stores.

Chutneys and pickles

From India to China chutneys and pickles are made from local ingredients: fruit, vegetables, fish. Though there is no hard and fast rule and I wouldn't be dogmatic, chutneys are sweet and usually contain fruit, raisins and sugar; and pickles are acid.

Both vary in degree as far as pungency is concerned. Colonel Skinner's Indian chutney, from a recipe made famous by the founder of the renowned cavalry regiment Skinner's Horse, can leave you gasping for water and pop-eyed. So can many a pickle: chilli pickle, for instance, made entirely of chillis, is no titillator for the novice.

Pungent food grows on one, however, and I have seen diners with beads of sweat starting from their brows and tears running down their cheeks, tucking into hot curries with evident enjoyment.

Bhurtas

Bhurtas are an Indian speciality: they usually have mashed potato as a base and include chopped herbs, chopped onion, garlic etc.

Potato Bhurta

1 medium-sized onion	*1 teaspoon mustard oil*
1 green chilli	*Juice of a lemon or lime*
8 potatoes	*Salt to taste*

Boil the potatoes and mash them. Chop onion and chilli into small pieces and squeeze lemon or lime juice over them. Add salt and mix with mustard oil. Mix all this into the mashed potato and beat thoroughly. Mustard oil has a distinct flavour: if you dislike it, substitute a teaspoon of butter or some other oil.

Brinjal Bhurta

1 medium-sized onion	*2 large brinjals (aubergines=egg plants)*
1 green chilli	*1 teaspoon mustard oil*
Juice of a lemon or lime	*Salt to taste*

Prepare onion, chilli, juice, oil and salt as for potato *bhurta*. Bake the aubergines till the insides are soft. Roasting in the ashes of a coal or wood fire brings out the flavour better than any other way. When cooked, scoop out the insides and mix with the other ingredients.

Herring Bhurta

1 large herring	*Juice of a lemon or lime*
1 green or 2 red chillis	*1 large potato*
1 onion	*Salt to taste*

This is perhaps the tastiest of all *bhurtas*. Grill the herring and bone it. The skin adds flavour, though you can remove it.

Boil the potato till soft. Chop onion and chilli into tiny pieces. Mash potato and mix in onion, chilli, juice and salt. Mash herring with a fork and mix it with the other ingredients, adding the oil that has dripped from the herring during grilling. The oil will be absorbed and neutralized by the potato but adds flavour.

Tomato Bhurta

6 tomatoes	*1 onion*
¼ teaspoon chilli	*Juice of a lemon*
½ teaspoon mustard oil	*Pinch of ground ginger*
½ dozen leaves of mint	*Salt to taste*

Bake the tomatoes till their skins crack, then mash them with mint, chilli, ginger, mustard oil, onion and salt. Pour over this the lemon juice. Try mint with other *bhurtas* too.

Yogurt

In the West yogurt is nearly always sweetened with sugar or honey, or with some fruit flavouring. In the East this is unusual.

One of the advantages of yogurt is that in hot climates milk does not keep very long and quickly becomes contaminated; on the other hand, because of the heat, yogurt is easy to make and the *Bacillus acidophilus,* which cracks the milk to produce curds and whey, also protects it from harmful germs. It is either ladled on to curries after they have been served, or included in the cooking of some dishes. It is a revelation to those who have never eaten yogurt this way to find what a difference it makes. Yogurt lends piquancy to curries.

Yogurt can be made *easily* and *cheaply* at home without any expensive apparatus whatever:

1. Heat a pint of milk to 180°F – if you haven't got a kitchen thermometer, till the surface of the milk starts to wrinkle. Then take off the milk and allow it to cool to blood heat – that is, about 100°, or cool enough to dip your finger in without getting it burnt.

2. Take 1 or 2 teaspoons of yogurt from a shop-bought carton, pop it into the milk and swill it round.

3. Cover and stand in a warm corner of the kitchen or

in an airing cupboard. Or, better still, pour it into a wide-mouthed thermos flask. In 12 hours the yogurt should be set and quite firm. And for the next lot, take some of this and use as in stage 2, repeating the process. *But once it has set don't mix the yogurt, otherwise you'll just get a mess.* One woman whom I told how to make yogurt complained that it wouldn't stay set. 'And I always mix it thoroughly after it's made!' No wonder. Yogurt made this way is a quarter or a fifth the cost of shop-bought yogurt.

Coconut milk

Coconut milk is used in many Indian dishes, more in Bengal and South India than in the north and west, and widely in Ceylon, Burma, Malaysia, Indonesia and Indo-China.

Curries made with it have a distinctive flavour and fragrance, especially fish and prawn curries. The milk resides inside the coconut and can be extracted by punching a hole or making a crack in the shell.

If you can't buy a coconut–everyone doesn't want to buy a coconut in order to get the milk–you can make some by expressing it from the flesh, though this milk does not compare in flavour with that contained in the nut. It is, however, a fair second-best.

Put one third of a pound of dessicated coconut into a bowl and pour over it a cup of boiling water. When the water is cool squeeze the coconut with the fingers, or mash it with a wooden masher, till the water is thick and creamy; then strain off the liquid into a jug. Repeat the process with the same pulp. Both pressings can be used as stock in making fish curries. The more coconut you use, the thicker will be the milk.

The most fragrant milk is made by buying a coconut and scraping the pulp from the nut with a specially designed scraper called a *khoornee,* which can be bought from an Indian spice shop; but only when the original milk has been used.

7. What does one drink with curries?

One is oftened asked: 'What are the right wines to go with curries?'

There is no straightforward answer, for drinks and drinking habits vary throughout the Orient. India has no wines or spirits of her own. In imperial India rum was distilled in places like Shahjehanpur and beer was brewed in Murree and elsewhere for British troops. Arrack (Arabic, sweet juice) is made illicitly from the milk of the coconut and the sap of the date tree; and in the days of the British Raj a fiery, potent liquor was made by soaking and fermenting hemp, jute or cotton waste and other products and sold in grog shops. And stinking stuff it was! Such places were shunned by respectable Hindu and Moslem alike. Today India is a 'dry' country and alcoholic stimulants are dispensed only to foreigners and the sick.

In any case, Indians don't drink when eating. If curries are too pungent, liquid does little to assuage the burning pangs. Rice or bread serves far better. Incidentally, long drinks with rice are not advisable as they create a feeling of fullness. After a meal, when betel, cardamom and a little *paan* (a pungent leaf of the cress family) have been chewed to clean the teeth, sweeten the breath and aid digestion, Indians usually sip glasses of sherbet (Arabic, *sharbah* from *shariba,* to drink; or Hindi, *sharbat*) or cups of spiced tea.

Originally sherbet was made from fruit juice and snow; but today from any fruit juice cooled, sweetened and sometimes flavoured with rose water. Indian sherbet bears no resemblance to the fizzy concoctions sold to children under that name elsewhere. The most popular sherbets are made from mango, *bael* (wood apple), palm fruit, pineapple, lime etc. Lemon is a good substitute for lime.

Spiced teas usually have a cinnamon, cardamom or mint base, for all three are tonics and digestives. Gerard, the famous physician and herbalist, wrote: 'The smell [of mint] rejoiceth the heart of man.' Spiced teas are taken hot or cold and flavoured with lime, lemon or cloves, and in a hot climate are refreshing.

Tea, of course, is drunk throughout the East. So are a variety of delicious fruit drinks made from the juice of local fruits: palm of various kinds, pineapple, *bael,* mango etc. The juice is crushed, sweetened and diluted, or else fermented into alcoholic liquor. Date palm juice is fermented into toddy.

The Japanese drink *sake,* made from rice, which contains 15-18% alcohol and bears a vague resemblance to sherry. Chinese wine is similar. In Malaysia Chinese wine *(shaohsing)* is used for cooking, Triple Distilled wine for social consumption, and Chinese rose wine for special occasions.

Suitable drinks to accompany curry in the West are a matter of taste. A good dry sherry goes well before an Indian meal. Try one of the 'finos': a pale Amontillado or a Manzanilla. Or if you prefer a sweet sherry, why not?

All light wines go with curries, white or red. Generally speaking such wines are the best beverages to drink with or after curries. Sweet, heavy wines do not go with curries; nor do spirits, which are much too fiery. Light beers and lagers are suitable, though being long drinks they are better before rather than with or after a meal.

If made with the right ingredients and kept for at least a year – two years is much better – many home-made wines can rival commercial light wines. A good elderberry wine resembles Burgundy, and hawthorn and elderflower wines are unbeatable. I gave a friend, who had lived for 18 years in France, a glass of elderflower and asked him what it was. He held it to the light, sniffed it, ran it round his palate, and then not only declared that it was superb but named the château that produced it!

Appendix: Curry Powder Ingredients

You can of course make up an infinite variety of curry powders from the available spices and herbs. Shown below, however, are my recommended ingredients for the powders used with the recipes in this book. Quantities are given as measured *after* grinding except for Pakistan, where spices can be used whole when cooked in a muslin bag.

INDIA

1 teaspoon turmeric
½ teaspoon cummin
½ teaspoon mustard seed
½ teaspoon fenugreek
2 teaspoons coriander
¼ teaspoon poppy seed
½ teaspoon ginger
¼ teaspoon chilli
*½ teaspoon black
    peppercorns*

PAKISTAN

5 whole cardamoms
5 whole cloves
5 black peppercorns
5 1-inch sticks cinnamon

BURMA

1 teaspoon ginger
½ teaspoon turmeric
1 teaspoon garlic powder
¼ teaspoon chilli

CEYLON

½ teaspoon fenugreek
2 teaspoons ginger
½ teaspoon turmeric
1 teaspoon garlic powder
1 teaspoon mustard seed
¾ teaspoon chilli

MALAYSIA

½ teaspoon ginger
¼ teaspoon garlic powder
1 teaspoon cinnamon
¼ teaspoon cloves
½ teaspoon cardamom
1 teaspoon turmeric
½ teaspoon chilli

VIETNAM

½ teaspoon chilli
½ teaspoon turmeric
¼ teaspoon black pepper
1 teaspoon ginger
½ teaspoon garlic powder

INDEX

Page numbers in bold type indicate recipes or major references